The 'How to Pray'
Guided Prayer Journal

Harvested Works Group LLC
8584 Washington St., #2015
Chagrin Falls, OH 44023-5369

ISBN Number: 978-1-7375908-3-5

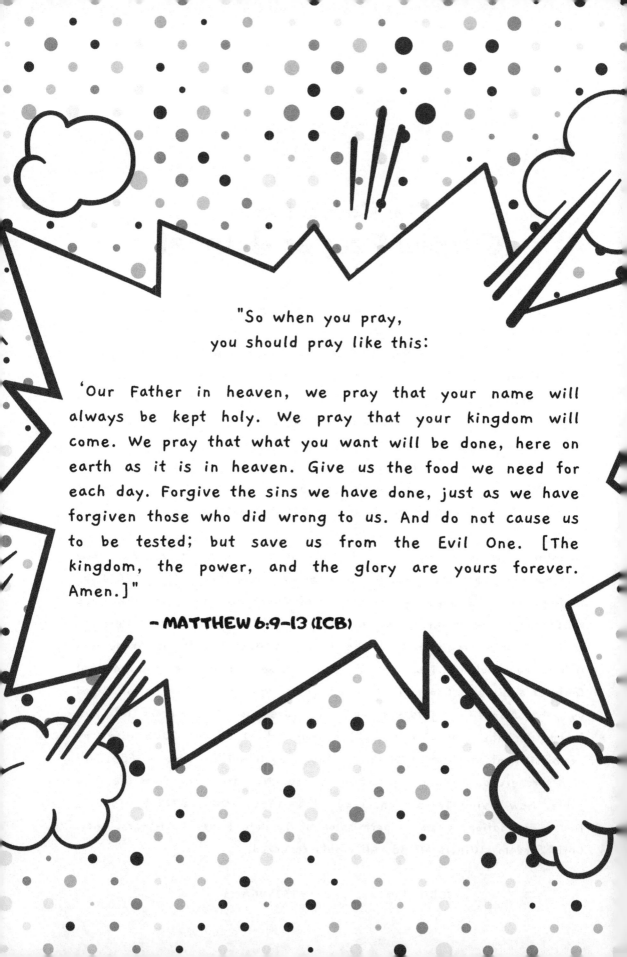

"So when you pray,
you should pray like this:

'Our Father in heaven, we pray that your name will always be kept holy. We pray that your kingdom will come. We pray that what you want will be done, here on earth as it is in heaven. Give us the food we need for each day. Forgive the sins we have done, just as we have forgiven those who did wrong to us. And do not cause us to be tested; but save us from the Evil One. [The kingdom, the power, and the glory are yours forever. Amen.]"

— MATTHEW 6:9–13 (ICB)

Train Up Arrows Presents:

The 'How to Pray'

Guided Prayer Journal

For Kids

A 12-Week Journey to God

by Tatiana Zurowski

This journal belongs to :

Hey there young arrow of faith! Welcome to
your very own Prayer Journal, a special place
where you can journey closer to God through
prayer (talking to Him). I'm thrilled you've
decided to embark on this spiritual adventure.
Let's dive in and discover the wonders that
await within these pages!

ALL ABOUT ME

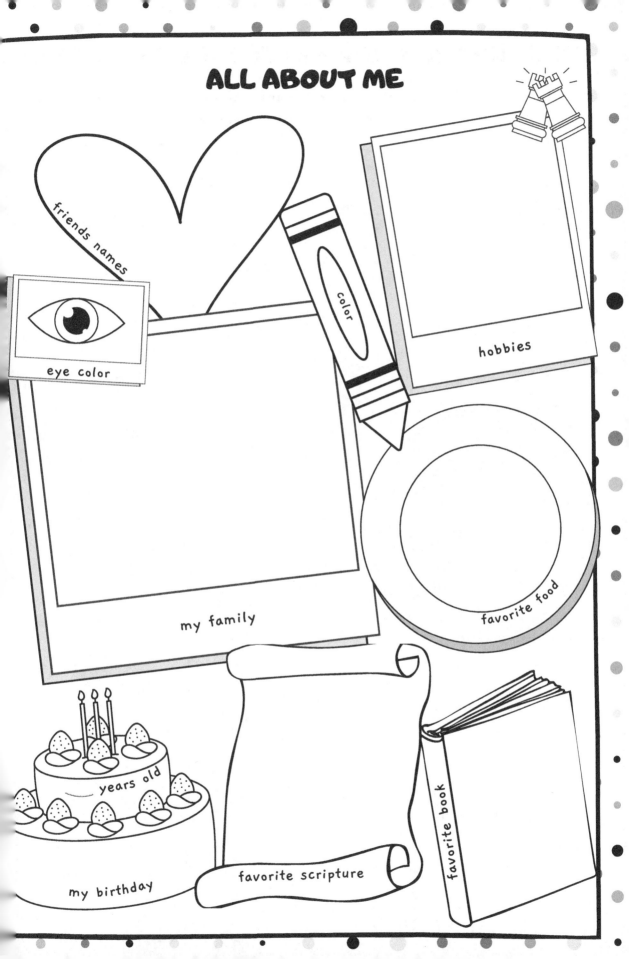

friends names

eye color

color

hobbies

my family

favorite food

years old

my birthday

favorite scripture

favorite book

THE HOW TO PRAY – FIVE FINGER METHOD

Let's learn how to use each finger and even the palm of your hand to make your prayers special and meaningful.

ADORATION
– Expressing your amazement about who God is
(Psalm 150:6)

CONFESSION
– Admitting your sins to God
(1 John 1:9)

THANKSGIVING
– Thanking God for all he has done in your life
(Psalm 9:1)

SUPPLICATION
– Praying for others
(1 Timothy 2:1-2)

PETITION
– Praying for your wants and needs
(Mark 11:24)

CLOSING
– End your prayer with Amen
(1 Chronicles 16:36)

"First of all, then, I urge that supplications, prayers, intercessions, and thanksgivings be made for all people."
- 1 Timothy 2:1 (NIV)

FIVE FINGER METHOD BREAKDOWN

When you want to talk to God, use this method to help you think of things to say.

PRAISE

Say nice things about God, to God.

ex. "Lord, you're so incredible! You made the world and everything in it!"

CONFESS

Tell God about the wrong things you've thought, said or done.

ex. "God, I apologize for being unkind to my sibling. Please forgive me."

THANKS

Thank God for all He's done for you or others.

ex. "Thank you Jesus for waking me up today."

OTHERS

Pray for other people. They can be strangers, family, friends or people you know.

ex. "I pray everyone learns to love each other."

YOU

Pray for yourself. Whatever you want, need or would like to have.

ex. "Father, please help me do well on my math test."

AMEN

Finally, say "Amen." Amen means, I agree.

It is like saying, "God, I trust that you heard my prayers, and I'm ready to follow your guidance."

BEING PRAYERFUL...

☑ invites more peace and joy into your life

☑ shifts our focus to others

☑ reduces feelings of isolation, anxiety and fear

☑ fosters a sense of connection

☑ strengthens your relationship to God

☑ increases gratitude and thankfulness

☑ blesses you, your family, and everyone you pray for

☑ helps you hear from God and learn about His plans for you

Tips to Use Your Prayer Journal:

There are no rules. There are no right or wrong ways to use this journal or pray. Praying is like talking to a Heavenly Father who can't be seen but is always there to listen. You can share your thoughts, feelings, dreams, worries, wishes, and thanks. It's a way to feel close to God. Just talk to Him like a loving Father and know that He cares for you a lot! Here are a few tips to help you get started.

1. Begin with an open heart: Before you write, close your eyes and say hello to God in your heart.
2. Find a Cozy Spot: Go to a quiet, comfy place where you feel close to God.
3. Write and Draw: You can write your thoughts and even draw pictures.
4. Use the Questions: There are questions in this journal, to help you talk to God.
5. Be Creative: Use colors, draw fun pictures, or tape in photos.
6. Listen Carefully: After you talk to God, listen in your heart for what He might say.

Ready? Grab your favorite pencil, take a deep breath, and let's talk to God. He is excited to listen!

With love,
Tatiana Zurowski

p.s. Feel free to use stickers, colors, and your imagination to make this journal uniquely yours. And always remember, God loves you more than you can imagine!

Daily Prayer Example

Date: 10/23/23

S (M) T W TH F S

How I Feel

Weather

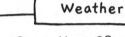

DEAR GOD,

Praises About God:

You are amazing and do wonderful things. You are super strong, and always there to help me!

Sins I Confess to God:

Lord, I apologize for being mean to my brother and sisters. I know I can do better, please forgive me and help me to be a better sibling.

Who Can I Pray For:

God, please help those who are hungry and don't have enough to eat. Help them find food and comfort.

I Thank God For:

Thank you, Jesus, for the toys that are fun to play with, they make me happy.

Things I Want / Need:

Heavenly Father, help me be kind and make good choices today.

AMEN!

Bi-Weekly Reflection Example

It's time to think about your week!

What made you happy while talking to God?

Being able to tell all my secrets to my best friend, and sometimes, I felt warm inside, like I was getting a big hug from God.

Was there anything that made it hard for you to pray? What was it?

Sometimes it was hard to pray when I was super excited about playing or doing fun stuff. My brain got all jumpy, and I got distracted. But Mama helped me, and we talked to God together.

Setting prayer goals are important so we can keep improving.

Goals for the Next 2 Weeks:

I want to remember to thank God every night, even when I'm super sleepy and maybe try to sit still for a bit longer.

Memory Verse:

"I will praise you as long as I live, and in your name I will lift up my hands."
-Psalm 63:4 (NIV)

Monthly Affirmations:

1. I will praise God my whole life

2. I lift my hands in joy

3. Write your own affirmation

Things I Learned:

I learned that when I talk to God, it's not just about asking for things. I can also say nice things about God, thank Him, and pray for others.

We learn all the time! What did you learn about prayer?

Daily Prayer

Date: _____   S M T W TH F S

How I Feel

Weather

DEAR GOD,

Praises About God:

Sins I Confess to God:

Who Can I Pray For:

I Thank God For:

Things I Want / Need:

AMEN!

Daily Prayer

Date: _____   S   M   T   W   TH   F   S

How I Feel

Weather

DEAR GOD,

Praises About God:

Sins I Confess to God:

Who Can I Pray For:

I Thank God For:

_____

_____

_____

_____

Things I Want / Need:

_____

_____

_____

AMEN!

Daily Prayer

Date: _____

S M T W TH F S

How I Feel

Weather

DEAR GOD,

Praises About God:

Sins I Confess to God:

Who Can I Pray For:

I Thank God For:

Things I Want / Need:

AMEN!

Daily Prayer

Date: _____   S   M   T   W   TH   F   S

How I Feel

Weather

DEAR GOD,

Praises About God:

Sins I Confess to God:

Who Can I Pray For:

I Thank God For:

Things I Want / Need:

AMEN!

Daily Prayer

Date: _____   S M T W TH F S

How I Feel

Weather

DEAR GOD,

Praises About God:

Sins I Confess to God:

Who Can I Pray For:

I Thank God For:

Things I Want / Need:

AMEN!

Daily Prayer

Date: _____   S M T W TH F S

How I Feel

Weather

DEAR GOD,

Praises About God:

Sins I Confess to God:

Who Can I Pray For:

I Thank God For:

Things I Want / Need:

AMEN!

Daily Prayer

Date: _____   S   M   T   W   TH   F   S

How I Feel

Weather

DEAR GOD,

Praises About God:

Sins I Confess to God:

Who Can I Pray For:

I Thank God For:

Things I Want / Need:

AMEN!

Daily Prayer

Date: _____ S M T W TH F S

How I Feel

Weather

DEAR GOD,

Praises About God:

Sins I Confess to God:

Who Can I Pray For:

I Thank God For:

_____

_____

_____

Things I Want / Need:

_____

_____

_____

AMEN!

Daily Prayer

Date: _____   S   M   T   W   TH   F   S

How I Feel

Weather

DEAR GOD,

Praises About God:

Sins I Confess to God:

Who Can I Pray For:

I Thank God For:

Things I Want / Need:

AMEN!

Daily Prayer

Date: _____   S M T W TH F S

How I Feel

Weather

DEAR GOD,

Praises About God:

Sins I Confess to God:

Who Can I Pray For:

I Thank God For:

_____

_____

_____

_____

Things I Want / Need:

_____

_____

_____

AMEN!

Daily Prayer

Date: _____   S M T W TH F S

How I Feel

Weather

DEAR GOD,

Praises About God:

Sins I Confess to God:

Who Can I Pray For:

I Thank God For:

_____

_____

_____

Things I Want / Need:

_____

_____

_____

AMEN!

Daily Prayer

Date: _____   S M T W TH F S

How I Feel

Weather

DEAR GOD,

Praises About God:

Sins I Confess to God:

Who Can I Pray For:

I Thank God For:

Things I Want / Need:

AMEN!

Daily Prayer

Date: _____   S M T W TH F S

How I Feel

Weather

DEAR GOD,

Praises About God:

Sins I Confess to God:

Who Can I Pray For:

I Thank God For:

_____
_____
_____

Things I Want / Need:

_____
_____
_____

AMEN!

Daily Prayer

Date: _____

S M T W TH F S

How I Feel

Weather

DEAR GOD,

Praises About God:

Sins I Confess to God:

Who Can I Pray For:

I Thank God For:

Things I Want / Need:

AMEN!

DATE: _____   S   M   T   W   TH   F   S

Bi-Weekly Reflection

It's time to think about your week!

What made you happy while talking to God?

Was there anything that made it hard for you to pray? What was it?

Goals for the Next 2 Weeks:

Setting prayer goals are important so we can keep improving.

Memory Verse:

"I will praise you as long as I live, and in your name I will lift up my hands."

-Psalm 63:4 (NIV)

Monthly Affirmations:

1. I will praise God my whole life

2. I thank God & lift my hands in joy

3. _____

Things I Learned:

We lear all the time! What di you lear about prayer?

WOW! GOD LISTENED!

"God listens when we pray, He hears us every day. So with thankful hearts, let's say, God listens when we pray." -Psalm 66:19

Prayers Answered   Date Answered

_____

_____

_____

THANK YOU GOD!

Daily Prayer

Date: _____   S M T W TH F S

How I Feel

Weather

DEAR GOD,

Praises About God:

Sins I Confess to God:

Who Can I Pray For:

I Thank God For:

Things I Want / Need:

AMEN!

Daily Prayer

Date: _____   S M T W TH F S

How I Feel

Weather

DEAR GOD,

Praises About God:

Sins I Confess to God:

Who Can I Pray For:

I Thank God For:

_____

_____

_____

Things I Want / Need:

_____

_____

_____

AMEN!

Daily Prayer

Date: _____   S M T W TH F S

How I Feel

Weather

DEAR GOD,

Praises About God:

Sins I Confess to God:

Who Can I Pray For:

I Thank God For:

Things I Want / Need:

AMEN!

Daily Prayer

Date: _____   S M T W TH F S

How I Feel

Weather

DEAR GOD,

Praises About God:

Sins I Confess to God:

Who Can I Pray For:

I Thank God For:

Things I Want / Need:

AMEN!

Daily Prayer

Date: _____   S M T W TH F S

How I Feel

Weather

DEAR GOD,

Praises About God:

Sins I Confess to God:

Who Can I Pray For:

I Thank God For:

Things I Want / Need:

AMEN!

Daily Prayer

Date: _____   S   M   T   W   TH   F   S

How I Feel

Weather

DEAR GOD,

Praises About God:

Sins I Confess to God:

Who Can I Pray For:

I Thank God For:

Things I Want / Need:

AMEN!

Daily Prayer

Date: _____   S M T W TH F S

How I Feel

Weather

DEAR GOD,

Praises About God:

Sins I Confess to God:

Who Can I Pray For:

I Thank God For:

_____

_____

_____

Things I Want / Need:

_____

_____

_____

AMEN!

Daily Prayer

Date: _____   S   M   T   W   TH   F   S

How I Feel

Weather

DEAR GOD,

Praises About God:

Sins I Confess to God:

Who Can I Pray For:

I Thank God For:

Things I Want / Need:

AMEN!

Daily Prayer

Date: _____   S   M   T   W   TH   F   S

How I Feel

Weather

DEAR GOD,

Praises About God:

Sins I Confess to God:

Who Can I Pray For:

I Thank God For:

Things I Want / Need:

AMEN!

Daily Prayer

Date: _____   S   M   T   W   TH   F   S

How I Feel

Weather

DEAR GOD,

Praises About God:

Sins I Confess to God:

Who Can I Pray For:

I Thank God For:

_____

_____

_____

Things I Want / Need:

_____

_____

_____

AMEN!

Daily Prayer

Date: _____   S M T W TH F S

How I Feel

Weather

DEAR GOD,

Praises About God:

Sins I Confess to God:

Who Can I Pray For:

I Thank God For:

_____
_____
_____
_____

Things I Want / Need:

_____
_____
_____

AMEN!

Daily Prayer

Date: _____   S   M   T   W   TH   F   S

How I Feel

Weather

DEAR GOD,

Praises About God:

Sins I Confess to God:

Who Can I Pray For:

I Thank God For:

_____

_____

_____

Things I Want / Need:

_____

_____

_____

AMEN!

Daily Prayer

Date: _____   S M T W TH F S

How I Feel

Weather

DEAR GOD,

Praises About God:

Sins I Confess to God:

Who Can I Pray For:

I Thank God For:

Things I Want / Need:

AMEN!

Daily Prayer

Date: _____

S M T W TH F S

How I Feel

Weather

DEAR GOD,

Praises About God:

Sins I Confess to God:

Who Can I Pray For:

I Thank God For:

_____

_____

_____

Things I Want / Need:

_____

_____

_____

AMEN!

DATE: _____   S M T W TH F S

Bi-Weekly Reflection

It's time to think about your week!

What was the favorite part of your prayer time?

What's something you want to talk to God about but haven't?

Setting prayer goals are important so we can keep improving.

Goals for the Next 2 Weeks:

Memory Verse:

"But if we confess our sins, he will forgive our sins. We can trust God. He does what is right. He will make us clean from all the wrongs we have done."
-1 John 1:9 (ICB)

Monthly Affirmations:

1. I confess my sins and trust in God

2. I am forgiven

3. _____

Things I Learned:

We learn all the time! What did you learn about prayer?

WOW! GOD LISTENED!

"God listens when we pray, He hears us every day. So with thankful hearts, let's say, God listens when we pray." -Psalm 66:19

Prayers Answered _____ Date Answered

_____

_____

_____

THANK YOU GOD!

Daily Prayer

Date: _____   S M T W TH F S

How I Feel

Weather

DEAR GOD,

Praises About God:

Sins I Confess to God:

Who Can I Pray For:

I Thank God For:

Things I Want / Need:

AMEN!

Daily Prayer

Date: _____   S   M   T   W   TH   F   S

How I Feel

Weather

DEAR GOD,

Praises About God:

Sins I Confess to God:

Who Can I Pray For:

I Thank God For:

_____

_____

_____

Things I Want / Need:

_____

_____

_____

AMEN!

Daily Prayer

Date: _____   S M T W TH F S

How I Feel

Weather

DEAR GOD,

Praises About God:

Sins I Confess to God:

Who Can I Pray For:

I Thank God For:

_____
_____
_____
_____

Things I Want / Need:

_____
_____
_____

AMEN!

Daily Prayer

Date: _____

S M T W TH F S

How I Feel

Weather

DEAR GOD,

Praises About God:

Sins I Confess to God:

Who Can I Pray For:

I Thank God For:

Things I Want / Need:

AMEN!

Daily Prayer

Date: _____ S M T W TH F S

How I Feel

Weather

DEAR GOD,

Praises About God:

Sins I Confess to God:

Who Can I Pray For:

I Thank God For:

Things I Want / Need:

AMEN!

Daily Prayer

Date: _____

S   M   T   W   TH   F   S

How I Feel

Weather

DEAR GOD,

Praises About God:

Sins I Confess to God:

Who Can I Pray For:

I Thank God For:

Things I Want / Need:

AMEN!

Daily Prayer

Date: _____   S M T W TH F S

How I Feel

Weather

DEAR GOD,

Praises About God:

Sins I Confess to God:

Who Can I Pray For:

I Thank God For:

Things I Want / Need:

AMEN!

Daily Prayer

Date: _____   S   M   T   W   TH   F   S

How I Feel

Weather

DEAR GOD,

Praises About God:

Sins I Confess to God:

Who Can I Pray For:

I Thank God For:

_____

_____

_____

_____

Things I Want / Need:

_____

_____

_____

AMEN!

Daily Prayer

Date: _____ S M T W TH F S

How I Feel

Weather

DEAR GOD,

Praises About God:

Sins I Confess to God:

Who Can I Pray For:

I Thank God For:

Things I Want / Need:

AMEN!

Daily Prayer

Date: _____   S   M   T   W   TH   F   S

How I Feel

Weather

DEAR GOD,

Praises About God:

Sins I Confess to God:

Who Can I Pray For:

I Thank God For:

_____

_____

_____

Things I Want / Need:

_____

_____

_____

AMEN!

Daily Prayer

Date: _____   S M T W TH F S

How I Feel

Weather

DEAR GOD,

Praises About God:

Sins I Confess to God:

Who Can I Pray For:

I Thank God For:

Things I Want / Need:

AMEN!

Daily Prayer

Date: _____   S M T W TH F S

How I Feel

Weather

DEAR GOD,

Praises About God:

Sins I Confess to God:

Who Can I Pray For:

I Thank God For:

_____
_____
_____
_____

Things I Want / Need:

_____
_____
_____

AMEN!

Daily Prayer

Date: _____   S M T W TH F S

How I Feel

😠 😢 😠 😐 🙂

Weather

DEAR GOD,

Praises About God:

Sins I Confess to God:

Who Can I Pray For:

I Thank God For:

_____

_____

_____

_____

Things I Want / Need:

_____

_____

_____

AMEN!

Daily Prayer

Date: _____ S M T W TH F S

How I Feel

Weather

DEAR GOD,

Praises About God:

Sins I Confess to God:

Who Can I Pray For:

I Thank God For:

_____

_____

_____

Things I Want / Need:

_____

_____

_____

AMEN!

DATE: _____   S M T W TH F S

Bi-Weekly Reflection

It's time to think about your week!

How did you feel when you talked to God in prayer?

Did you listen for God's voice or feelings in your heart when you prayed?

Setting prayer goals are important so we can keep improving.

Goals for the Next 2 Weeks:

Memory Verse:

"I will give thanks to you, Lord, with all my heart; I will tell of all your wonderful deeds."
-Psalm 9:1 (NIV)

Monthly Affirmations:

1. I will thank God with all my heart

2. I will speak of God's goodness

3. _____

Things I Learned:

We learn all the time! What did you learn about prayer?

WOW! GOD LISTENED!

"God listens when we pray, He hears us every day. So with thankful hearts, let's say, God listens when we pray." -Psalm 66:19

Prayers Answered _____ Date Answered

_____

_____

_____

THANK YOU GOD!

Daily Prayer

Date: _____   S   M   T   W   TH   F   S

How I Feel

Weather

DEAR GOD,

Praises About God:

Sins I Confess to God:

Who Can I Pray For:

I Thank God For:

Things I Want / Need:

AMEN!

Daily Prayer

Date: _____   S   M   T   W   TH   F   S

How I Feel

Weather

DEAR GOD,

Praises About God:

Sins I Confess to God:

Who Can I Pray For:

I Thank God For:

_____

_____

_____

Things I Want / Need:

_____

_____

_____

AMEN!

Daily Prayer

Date: _____   S M T W TH F S

How I Feel

Weather

DEAR GOD,

Praises About God:

Sins I Confess to God:

Who Can I Pray For:

I Thank God For:

_____

_____

_____

Things I Want / Need:

_____

_____

_____

AMEN!

Daily Prayer

Date: _____   S   M   T   W   TH   F   S

How I Feel

Weather

DEAR GOD,

Praises About God:

Sins I Confess to God:

Who Can I Pray For:

I Thank God For:

_____

_____

_____

Things I Want / Need:

_____

_____

_____

AMEN!

Daily Prayer

Date: _____   S M T W TH F S

How I Feel

Weather

DEAR GOD,

Praises About God:

Sins I Confess to God:

Who Can I Pray For:

I Thank God For:

Things I Want / Need:

AMEN!

Daily Prayer

Date: _____   S   M   T   W   TH   F   S

How I Feel

Weather

DEAR GOD,

Praises About God:

Sins I Confess to God:

Who Can I Pray For:

I Thank God For:

_____

_____

_____

Things I Want / Need:

_____

_____

_____

AMEN!

Daily Prayer

Date: _____   S   M   T   W   TH   F   S

How I Feel

Weather

DEAR GOD,

Praises About God:

Sins I Confess to God:

Who Can I Pray For:

I Thank God For:

Things I Want / Need:

AMEN!

Daily Prayer

Date: _____

S M T W TH F S

How I Feel

Weather

DEAR GOD,

Praises About God:

Sins I Confess to God:

Who Can I Pray For:

I Thank God For:

Things I Want / Need:

AMEN!

Daily Prayer

Date: _____ S M T W TH F S

How I Feel

Weather

DEAR GOD,

Praises About God:

Sins I Confess to God:

Who Can I Pray For:

I Thank God For:

Things I Want / Need:

AMEN!

Daily Prayer

Date: _____   S M T W TH F S

How I Feel

Weather

DEAR GOD,

Praises About God:

Sins I Confess to God:

Who Can I Pray For:

I Thank God For:

_____
_____
_____

Things I Want / Need:

_____
_____
_____

AMEN!

Daily Prayer

Date: _____   S M T W TH F S

How I Feel

Weather

DEAR GOD,

Praises About God:

Sins I Confess to God:

Who Can I Pray For:

I Thank God For:

Things I Want / Need:

AMEN!

Daily Prayer

Date: _____   S M T W TH F S

How I Feel

Weather

DEAR GOD,

Praises About God:

Sins I Confess to God:

Who Can I Pray For:

I Thank God For:

Things I Want / Need:

AMEN!

Daily Prayer

Date: _____   S M T W TH F S

How I Feel

Weather

DEAR GOD,

Praises About God:

Sins I Confess to God:

Who Can I Pray For:

I Thank God For:

Things I Want / Need:

AMEN!

Daily Prayer

Date: _____

S M T W TH F S

How I Feel

Weather

DEAR GOD,

Praises About God:

Sins I Confess to God:

Who Can I Pray For:

I Thank God For:

_____

_____

_____

Things I Want / Need:

_____

_____

_____

AMEN!

DATE: _____

Bi-Weekly Reflection

It's time to think about your week!

What was the most special thing about your time talking to God?

How has praying changed the way you think of God, yourself or others?

Setting prayer goals are important so we can keep improving.

Goals for the Next 2 Weeks:

Memory Verse:

"I ask you to pray for all people. Ask God to bless them and give them what they need. And give thanks. You should pray for rulers and for all who have authority. Pray for those who persecute you."
-1 Timothy 2:1-2

Monthly Affirmations:

1. I pray for all people

2. My prayers make the world better

3. _____

Things I Learned:

We learn all the time! What did you learn about prayer?

WOW! GOD LISTENED!

"God listens when we pray, He hears us every day. So with thankful hearts, let's say, God listens when we pray." -Psalm 66:19

Prayers Answered   Date Answered

_____

_____

_____

THANK YOU GOD!

Daily Prayer

Date: _____   S M T W TH F S

How I Feel

Weather

DEAR GOD,

Praises About God:

Sins I Confess to God:

Who Can I Pray For:

I Thank God For:

Things I Want / Need:

AMEN!

Daily Prayer

Date: _____

S M T W TH F S

How I Feel

Weather

DEAR GOD,

Praises About God:

Sins I Confess to God:

Who Can I Pray For:

I Thank God For:

_____

_____

_____

Things I Want / Need:

_____

_____

_____

AMEN!

Daily Prayer

Date: _____

S M T W TH F S

How I Feel

Weather

DEAR GOD,

Praises About God:

Sins I Confess to God:

Who Can I Pray For:

I Thank God For:

_____

_____

_____

Things I Want / Need:

_____

_____

_____

AMEN!

Daily Prayer

Date: _____   S M T W TH F S

How I Feel

Weather

DEAR GOD,

Praises About God:

Sins I Confess to God:

Who Can I Pray For:

I Thank God For:

Things I Want / Need:

AMEN!

Daily Prayer

Date: _____ S M T W TH F S

How I Feel

Weather

DEAR GOD,

Praises About God:

Sins I Confess to God:

Who Can I Pray For:

I Thank God For:

Things I Want / Need:

AMEN!

Daily Prayer

Date: _____ S M T W TH F S

How I Feel

Weather

DEAR GOD,

Praises About God:

Sins I Confess to God:

Who Can I Pray For:

I Thank God For:

Things I Want / Need:

AMEN!

Daily Prayer

Date: _____   S   M   T   W   TH   F   S

How I Feel

Weather

DEAR GOD,

Praises About God:

Sins I Confess to God:

Who Can I Pray For:

I Thank God For:

_____
_____
_____
_____

Things I Want / Need:

_____
_____
_____

AMEN!

Daily Prayer

Date: _____

S M T W TH F S

How I Feel

Weather

DEAR GOD,

Praises About God:

Sins I Confess to God:

Who Can I Pray For:

I Thank God For:

Things I Want / Need:

AMEN!

Daily Prayer

Date: _____ S M T W TH F S

How I Feel

Weather

DEAR GOD,

Praises About God:

Sins I Confess to God:

Who Can I Pray For:

I Thank God For:

Things I Want / Need:

AMEN!

Daily Prayer

Date: _____   S M T W TH F S

How I Feel

Weather

DEAR GOD,

Praises About God:

Sins I Confess to God:

Who Can I Pray For:

I Thank God For:

_____

_____

_____

Things I Want / Need:

_____

_____

_____

AMEN!

Daily Prayer

Date: _____   S   M   T   W   TH   F   S

How I Feel

Weather

DEAR GOD,

Praises About God:

Sins I Confess to God:

Who Can I Pray For:

I Thank God For:

Things I Want / Need:

AMEN!

Daily Prayer

Date: _____   S   M   T   W   TH   F   S

How I Feel

Weather

DEAR GOD,

Praises About God:

Sins I Confess to God:

Who Can I Pray For:

I Thank God For:

Things I Want / Need:

AMEN!

Daily Prayer

Date: _____   S M T W TH F S

How I Feel

Weather

DEAR GOD,

Praises About God:

Sins I Confess to God:

Who Can I Pray For:

I Thank God For:

Things I Want / Need:

AMEN!

Daily Prayer

Date: _____   S   M   T   W   TH   F   S

How I Feel

Weather

DEAR GOD,

Praises About God:

Sins I Confess to God:

Who Can I Pray For:

I Thank God For:

Things I Want / Need:

AMEN!

DATE: _____

S   M   T   W   TH   F   S

Bi-Weekly Reflection

It's time to think about your week!

Has praying been easy or hard for you? Why?

How has talking to God in your prayers made you a better person?

Setting prayer goals are important so we can keep improving.

Goals for the Next 2 Weeks:

Memory Verse:

"Don't worry about anything;
instead, pray about everything.
Tell God what you need, and
thank Him for all he has done."
-Philippians 4:6 (NLT)

Monthly Affirmations:

1. I can talk to God about anything

2. God listens & helps me when I ask

3. _____

Things I Learned:

We learn all the time! What did you learn about prayer?

WOW! GOD LISTENED!

"God listens when we pray, He hears us every day. So with thankful hearts, let's say, God listens when we pray." -Psalm 66:19

Prayers Answered   Date Answered

_____

_____

_____

THANK YOU GOD!

Daily Prayer

Date: _____   S   M   T   W   TH   F   S

How I Feel

Weather

DEAR GOD,

Praises About God:

Sins I Confess to God:

Who Can I Pray For:

I Thank God For:

Things I Want / Need:

AMEN!

Daily Prayer

Date: _____   S M T W TH F S

How I Feel

Weather

DEAR
GOD,

Praises About God:

Sins I Confess to God:

Who Can I Pray For:

I Thank God For:

Things I Want / Need:

AMEN!

Daily Prayer

Date: _____   S M T W TH F S

How I Feel

Weather

DEAR GOD,

Praises About God:

Sins I Confess to God:

Who Can I Pray For:

I Thank God For:

Things I Want / Need:

AMEN!

Daily Prayer

Date: _____   S M T W TH F S

How I Feel

Weather

DEAR GOD,

Praises About God:

Sins I Confess to God:

Who Can I Pray For:

I Thank God For:

Things I Want / Need:

AMEN!

Daily Prayer

Date: _____   S M T W TH F S

How I Feel

Weather

DEAR GOD,

Praises About God:

Sins I Confess to God:

Who Can I Pray For:

I Thank God For:

Things I Want / Need:

AMEN!

Daily Prayer

Date: _____   S M T W TH F S

How I Feel

Weather

DEAR GOD,

Praises About God:

Sins I Confess to God:

Who Can I Pray For:

I Thank God For:

Things I Want / Need:

AMEN!

Daily Prayer

Date: _____   S   M   T   W   TH   F   S

How I Feel

Weather

DEAR GOD,

Praises About God:

Sins I Confess to God:

Who Can I Pray For:

I Thank God For:

Things I Want / Need:

AMEN!

Daily Prayer

Date: _____   S M T W TH F S

How I Feel

Weather

DEAR GOD,

Praises About God:

Sins I Confess to God:

Who Can I Pray For:

I Thank God For:

Things I Want / Need:

AMEN!

Daily Prayer

Date: _____   S   M   T   W   TH   F   S

How I Feel

Weather

DEAR GOD,

Praises About God:

Sins I Confess to God:

Who Can I Pray For:

I Thank God For:

Things I Want / Need:

AMEN!

Daily Prayer

Date: _____   S M T W TH F S

How I Feel

Weather

DEAR GOD,

Praises About God:

Sins I Confess to God:

Who Can I Pray For:

I Thank God For:

Things I Want / Need:

AMEN!

Daily Prayer

Date: _____ S M T W TH F S

How I Feel

Weather

DEAR GOD,

Praises About God:

Sins I Confess to God:

Who Can I Pray For:

I Thank God For:

Things I Want / Need:

AMEN!

Daily Prayer

Date: _____   S   M   T   W   TH   F   S

How I Feel

Weather

DEAR GOD,

Praises About God:

Sins I Confess to God:

Who Can I Pray For:

I Thank God For:

Things I Want / Need:

AMEN!

Daily Prayer

Date: _____   S   M   T   W   TH   F   S

How I Feel

Weather

DEAR GOD,

Praises About God:

Sins I Confess to God:

Who Can I Pray For:

I Thank God For:

Things I Want / Need:

AMEN!

Daily Prayer

Date: _____ S M T W TH F S

How I Feel

Weather

DEAR GOD,

Praises About God:

Sins I Confess to God:

Who Can I Pray For:

I Thank God For:

Things I Want / Need:

AMEN!

DATE: _____

S M T W TH F S

Bi-Weekly Reflection

It's time to think about your week!

What did you ask God for but are happy He said 'no'? Why?

How have your prayers changed over these 3 months?

Setting prayer goals are important so we can keep improving.

Goals for the Next 2 Weeks:

Memory Verse:

"We are sure that if we ask for anything He wants us to have, He will hear us. If we are sure He hears us when we ask, we can be sure He will give us what we ask for."

-1 John 5:14-15 (NLV)

Monthly Affirmations:

1. God hears my prayers

2. I believe God gives me whats best

3. _____

Things You Learned:

We learn all the time! What did you learn about prayer?

WOW! GOD LISTENED!

"God listens when we pray, He hears us every day. So with thankful hearts, let's say, God listens when we pray." -Psalm 66:19

Prayers Answered   Date Answered

_____

_____

_____

THANK YOU GOD!

Closing Prayer

Dear Heavenly Father,

Thank you for being with this arrow of faith as they finished writing in this prayer journal. I'm happy for the time they spent thinking about you, and your goodness while sharing those thoughts with you.

Lord, we're asking for your help as this young soul keeps on their spiritual journey. Please make your light shine on their path so they always know what's right. Give them strength when things get tough, courage when they're not sure, and help them stay connected with you through it all.

Bless this child with a heart that's full of love, kindness, and caring. Help them spread your love to others in a gentle way.

God, let them always feel happy and curious as they grow up. May they find joy in the simple moments, see the beauty in the world, and feel peaceful when they talk to you.

As they close the pages of this journal, let a brand-new chapter of incredible spiritual growth and discovery begin. Let all the good things they've learned here stick with them, forming a super strong relationship with you.

In your love and kindness, we're putting this awesome child in your hands, knowing you will continue to guide and protect them every step of the way. Thank you. God! In Jesus' name, I pray, Amen!

With Love,
Tatiana Zurowski

Made in the USA
Las Vegas, NV
23 January 2024

84798461R00063